Oklahomaography

FIRST EDITION, 2010
COPYRIGHT © 2010 BY JOEY BROWN
ALL RIGHTS RESERVED.
ISBN 978-0-9801684-6-4

No part of this book may be performed, recorded, or otherwise transmitted without the written consent of the author and the permission of the publisher. However, portions of poems may be cited for book reviews without obtaining consent.

Cover photo *Barbed Wire, Comanche* © 2009 by Joey Brown,
Cover design by Mongrel Empire Press

Text photos:
Hay Bale, Comanche © 2009 by Joey Brown
Packard, Meridian © 2009 by Joey Brown
Bridge, Redings Mill © 2009 by Bo Thomas Weast
Brick Wall, Comanche © 2009 by Joey Brown
Joey Brown © 2009 by Bo Thomas Weast

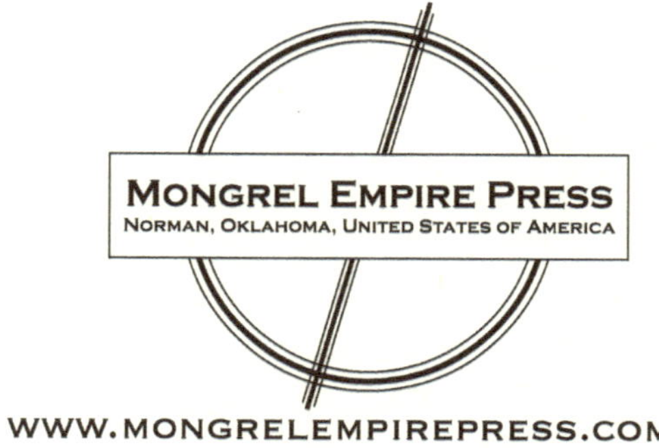

This publisher is a proud member of

[clmp]

COUNCIL OF LITERARY MAGAZINES & PRESSES
w w w . c l m p . o r g

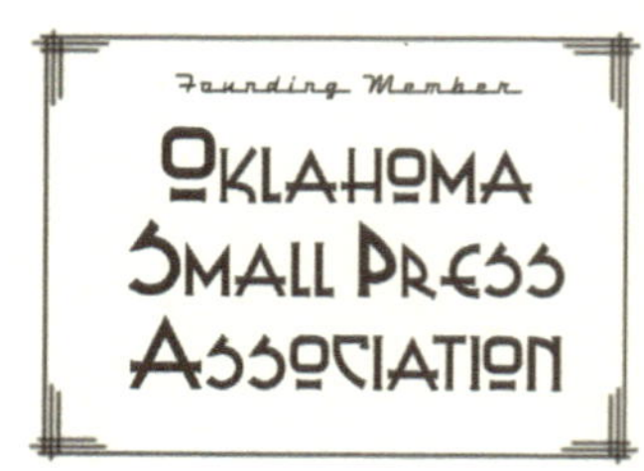

Book Design: Mongrel Empire Press using iWork Pages.

Oklahomaography

Joey Brown

MONGREL EMPIRE PRESS   NORMAN, OK

Acknowledgements

These poems originally appeared in the following publications:

"Maps, Pt. 2" *Paper Street*
"Geography Lessons" *Compass Rose*
"Pryor" *Argestes*
"Tornado Poem" *Argestes*
"Meridian, Oklahoma" *The Chaffin Journal*
"Louisiana" *Pinyon*
"Wind" *Ellipses*
"Maps to the Crash Sites" appeared in an earlier version in *The Dos Passos Review*

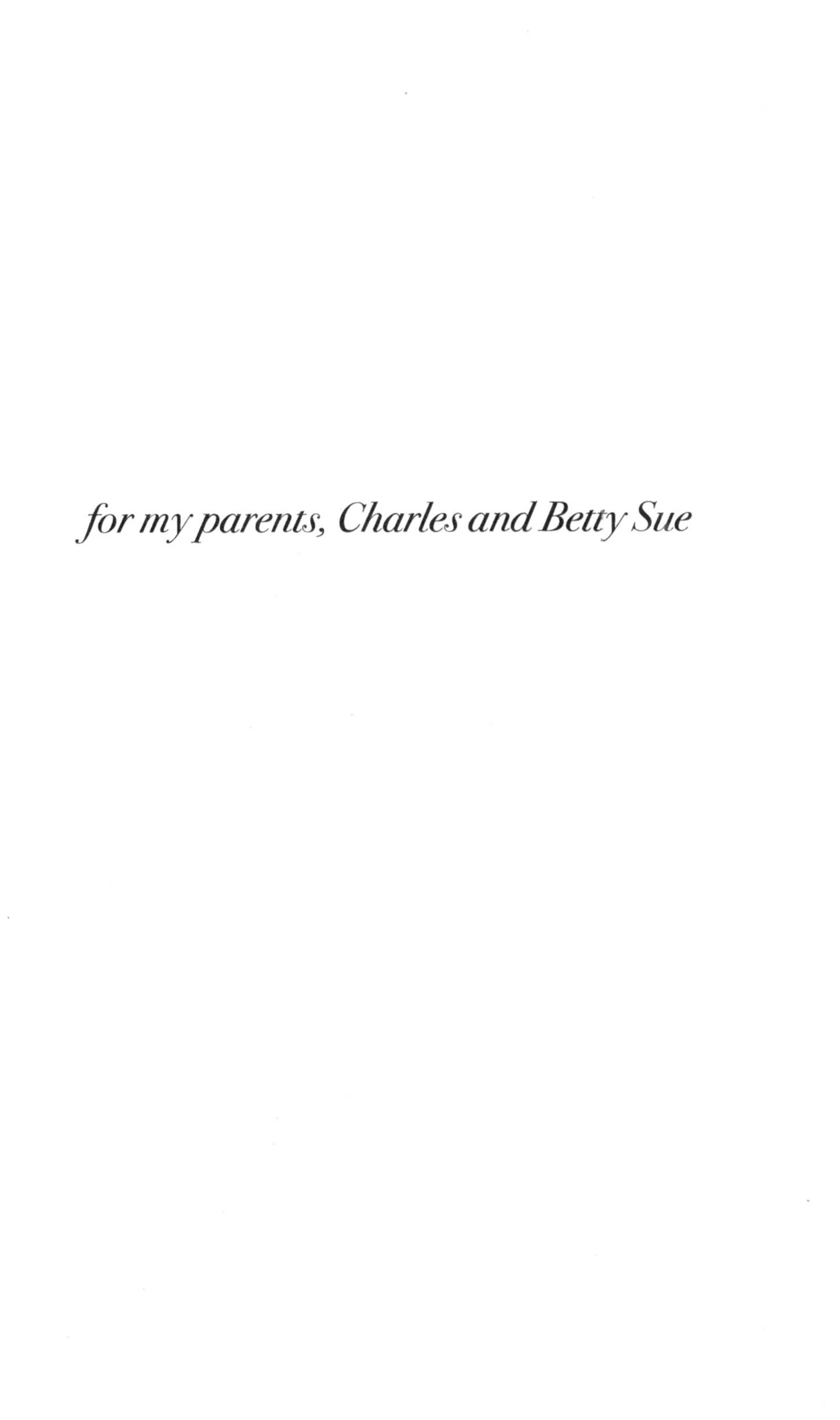

for my parents, Charles and Betty Sue

Contents

Contents

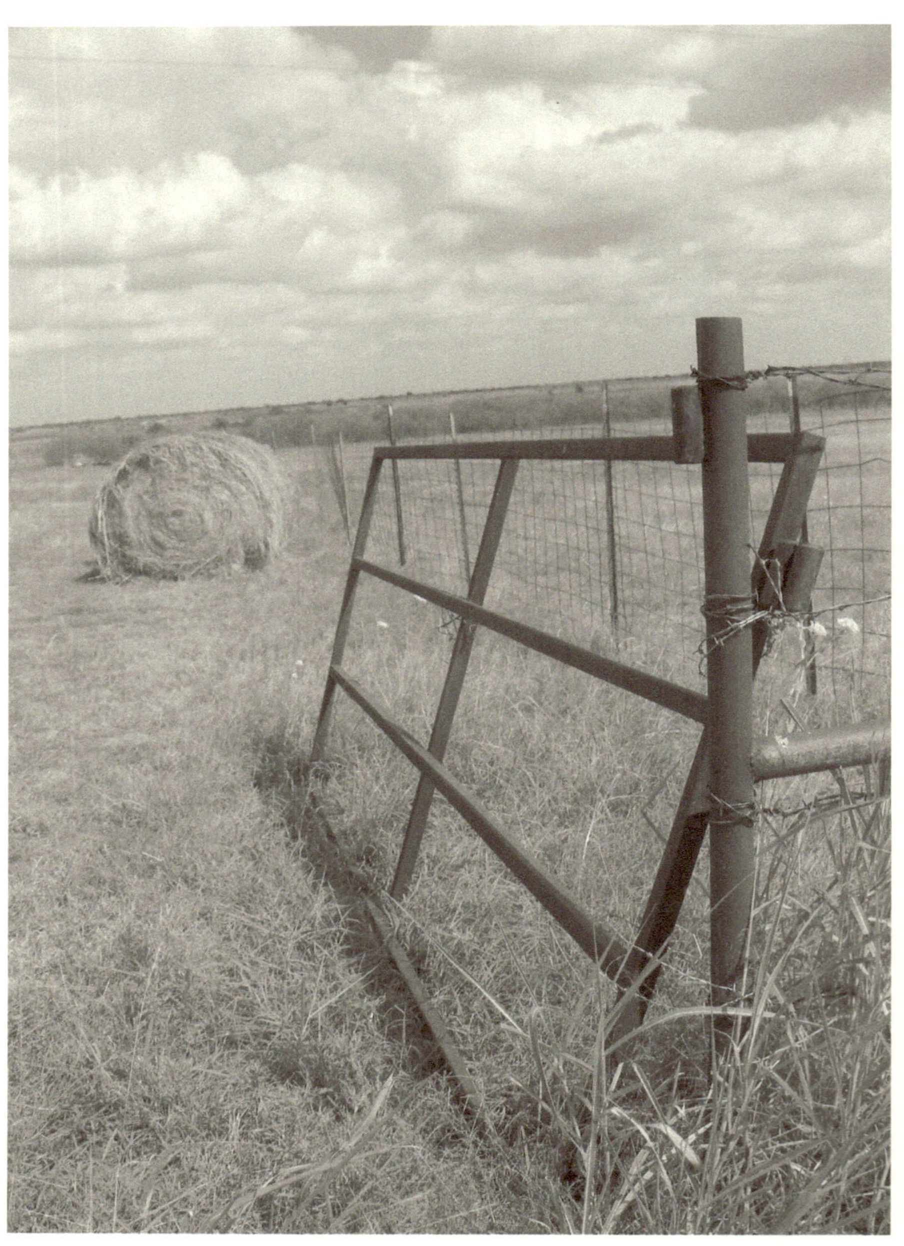

I Keep Saying Oklahoma

Lost in the Same Place Twice

when you go looking for it trouble's easy
enough and if you're gonna look out down
the road thataway you're gonna find nobody
to blame but yourself and then you'll be happy
for any excuse to slow down to sit down
and cry over the way quiet at night stirs
the tops of the trees how rainwater in the
barditches slips red and when you go
looking around again you'll find the
echo of the place empty and realize if
you don't see it you ought not believe
it's there lose the answer to how fast
can you go how fast you gotta go

Meridian, Oklahoma

Three boys wake up, in a town that's not really
a town, weighted down by the early morning summer.
They breathe in the sour sulphur from the refinery
that clanks and churns or whatever it is the refinery
does to make someone some little bit of money.
It's not them, not their houses, so what do they care
but for the nagging smell.

Three boys pump their bicycles on the highway
past the yard of rusted-up drill bits. You'd be afraid
for them were this a highway anywhere else. In the
convenience store they take two Cokes and an orange
Fanta out of the lay-down cooler. They like the pop &
sigh the bottle opener makes. When the door opens again,
the air conditioner pleads.

Three boys wait in the parking lot but don't know
they're waiting. Sit astride the bikes, bottles clinking
here and there, don't speak. They stare at the white day
reflecting off the school across the road, blistering their
eyes. You just know they don't imagine the size of all
they listen to. They can't. One of them keeps firecrackers
leftover in his pocket.

Tornado Poem

One little house is gone, the neighbor's:
that old man who drives the
blue truck with the camper shell
plastered with bumper stickers,
four from the Christian radio station.
Square house, good house. Been
here longer than any of us. Was.
Gone. Kindling the sum of it all.
The red plum/warm grease smell
of his kitchen still rests on the air.
Just like the devil to leave out
all the details. Ashy white spider,
undisturbed, in the blackberries out back.

Pryor

Count the miles and life there,
defined by living side-of-the-road.
Tomatoes, corn, honey, you can even
buy the bees. FOR SALE
GOATS, the word homegrown
squeezed in along the bottom.
A boy on horseback comes up the ditch,
bunch of younger ones walking behind.
They're carrying creek water
in a plastic cup, crawdads caught
with baloney and string. INDIAN:
TACOS JEWELRY ART
the sun too white to read
the rest. He's got a cowhide
slung over the fence, two red dogs
laying in the shade. Country music,
that's his favorite, real players,
truth in a line. You smell grease from
the café, taste sweat already dried.
You're going to make him an offer,
contemplate your life off the map.

Refinery Road

At five every day they opened the gates and the
workers came out. First in steady drips, then
clusters and streams, until men spewed from the
tall chain link. When the last man crossed out
the gates locked by a series of clasps so violent,
as if to say "we're done with you."

The men filed up the road carrying paper sacks
and lunchboxes and hardhats coated in grime.
Wore steel-toed boots, t-shirts that had once been
white, their coveralls turned down at the waist.
In the winter, Carhartt jackets new for Christmas.

Looking down they peeled off through the rows of
cracker box company houses. The only
choice was siding in blue or green. Yards set
here and there with swings and plywood
benches, yellow flowers suggesting the sun.

They wouldn't tell you what they did, except to
say the Fourth of July was never a workday. But
stand close and you'd see their white scars and
busted knuckles; smell rotten eggs and the far
off flavor of something like motor oil; hear the
chemical hiss of their collective exhale.

Dogs Come to Town

Legends of the spring, they started out a pack of
four ranging around the trash dump east of town.
They feasted on scraps, any old food that they found,
any manner of animal lesser than they. They
had speed, at least one half-coyote, all of them fierce,
muscled, and lean. Beasts, they stood wolfing
sentinels over heaps of broken furniture, tin
cans, and territory claimed. They snarled
all comers down from the gates, foam and
teeth like those of the devil. When enough
people got scared, started throwing trash in the
ditch, the sheriff took a shotgun to the hill.
But those dogs, sensing the shift in the seasons,
had long ago moved on. Across the highway
and onto the ranch, fewer visitors, bigger game.
They could smell it, my father said, when the
heifers started birthing so we kept an eye out
night and day. At the station Bill said "seen 'em in
town last night," standing by the back door of the
auto body shop. They turned on his truck, unfazed
by the engine, silently took surveillance. Absorbed
by the night if not for headlights glinting in their
eyes. Said when he looked back they were gone. No
abiding wild dogs without fear.

My father came upon them, already set on a heifer.
They got the calf before she was even done having it.
He pulled out a Winchester, fired once in their midst.
Black and white one went straight down. When he
put it dead in the bed of the pick-up, even shot, it just
looked like somebody's dog. Weakened by the loss
the pack broke down, every mad dog out for himself.
Within days they got one in the alley back of Strange's,
one more on the highway off the ridge. It's what you
gotta do when wild dogs come to town. Kill whatever

can't be loved out. Bill saw the last one, the half-
coyote, the leader, in the switchgrass on the low
pasture last July. He crawled with his gun, soldier-
style, mud caking his shirt, while he maneuvered
his way downwind. The breeze rocked the grass, lifted up
the animal's hair, and he imagined he saw it breathe.
But that dog was already dead. Fallen, swathed in peace.
Bill lay still alongside, heart thudding like a traitor,
some things natural you can't do nothing about.

Sunday

Men talk in the yard, as dressed up
as working men get: intentions clean
as their white pearl-snap shirts,
thoughts sharp as creases in their
Wranglers. From a long yellow
LTD the driver, in his own short-
sleeved Sunday shirt, points. Says
to watch out for that joker you can't
tell about him. They laugh as the car
slips on down Fifth even though they
don't know which one of them he
means. Aftershave mixes with rust
and clay on the air, teeth glint in
sun-worn faces. This is the only day
this week any of them will be like this.

A Girl You Could Get, Pt. 2

You're left with a picture,
more or less.
Small towns are just that way.
The every-day is special:
the parking lot of a fish joint
on the highway into Nocona,
she waits, her arm out the window,
fingers feeling for good air.
You're coming in, she's going out
in the direction of another country.
Back in her house she keeps
a stack of books where the tv would be.
She mentions the river
and the bridge thirty years in falling.

You're out of your depth,
sudden as it feels,
and you listen to the cicadas'
metronomic soundtrack
rather than think of the words you say.
She turns the car and you look:
the bone structure you've memorized
and all the traces of how true she is.
You think then you know:
summer, symbol,
the speed she will carry.

The Given End

Nothing good ever happens on a gravel road and when you live
in a cow town surrounded by them you can't help wilting
through a thousand summer days. What jobs we had
ended by eight, leaving determination enough to chase boredom down
one county road and then another, certain as we were that town,
with no movie theater or even a public pool table, had long ago
revealed to us the best it had to offer. We could make three dollars
worth of gas last all night and so sped along lines dissecting fields,
practiced as we were at going in every direction. It was not
unusual to intersect ourselves coming or going. It was all we had,
driving, and it was the same as life.

We abandoned the redundant hang-outs and a chunk of our
common sense, set out to see only those parts of Stephens County
visible from the interior of a '79 Ford Mustang. We counted off
the steakhouse, the cemetery, Sorrell's pecan orchard as we journeyed
landmark to landmark away from the scant excuse for civilization
to the pitch-black nether of the country. Even at a hundred degrees
we rolled the windows down and smelled hay cut that day, let the
grease hanging around the gas leases cling to our hair. The grind of
tires on gravel rode us hard so someone punched in some Van Halen,
and in the joining of tempos our fates were sealed.

Somewhere between adventure and stupidity we turned
the headlights off and allowed the guitar to accelerate
our fever to escape. The faster we went the deeper the washboard
roadway cut, our back wheels bumping a split second from
out-of-control. We topped a hill and braced against our stomachs
lurching, and then we sailed up the next hill and the next, our
stomachs falling harder on every drop. Not one of us could speak.
The wailing music and gory thud of metal denting as
gravel crashed into the wheel wells blurred into the rush of hot air
through the windows. Our bodies lifted from the seats just after
we crested each hill and just before the car reentered gravitational pull.
For brief fantastical seconds we hung suspended above the road,
above bit yards and refineries, above our lives as kids of an

impoverished oil town, and cradled for that one moment in the night
we got the feeling of what it would mean to be shed of this place.
We had elevated into foreign territory and gotten lost to total darkness.

Lights on or off, we would not have made the curve. The car wadded
into a ball of barbed wire fence that had seconds before separated
someone's pasture from fools like us. Then we were silent,
except for the collected exhalation of our breath and the cassette
player clicking onto "Runnin' With the Devil." Extracting ourselves
was easier done than explained, blind as we were miles beyond
streetlights. We wore the stings of broken windshield and fencing nails
and waded through the Johnson grass to the road. There we waited
for someone to come along and take us back, sure another
carload of souls resembling ours was at due any time. No one asked
if we were all right. We knew how we got there in the first place.

Oklahomaography

Standing in a museum of natural history I
locate myself. Study my hands, palms up and
fingers spread, read for the echo of what I
know to be the story of my flesh. For if it's
charted on a map it's true, no?

State outline carved in granite, genetic earth
in architectural splendor. Plains, water, roads,
schema of lines between good and lost. Same as
what is stained into my skin, spoken in the
hard syllables running from fingertip to wrist,
elbow to breath.

As far as I know being I know here. Topography
more physical than words, relief more wild than
lightning, features too fine to map. I come down here to
put my hand in the dirt. Taste it. Listen. No language to
manage what crossing the border breaks loose in me.

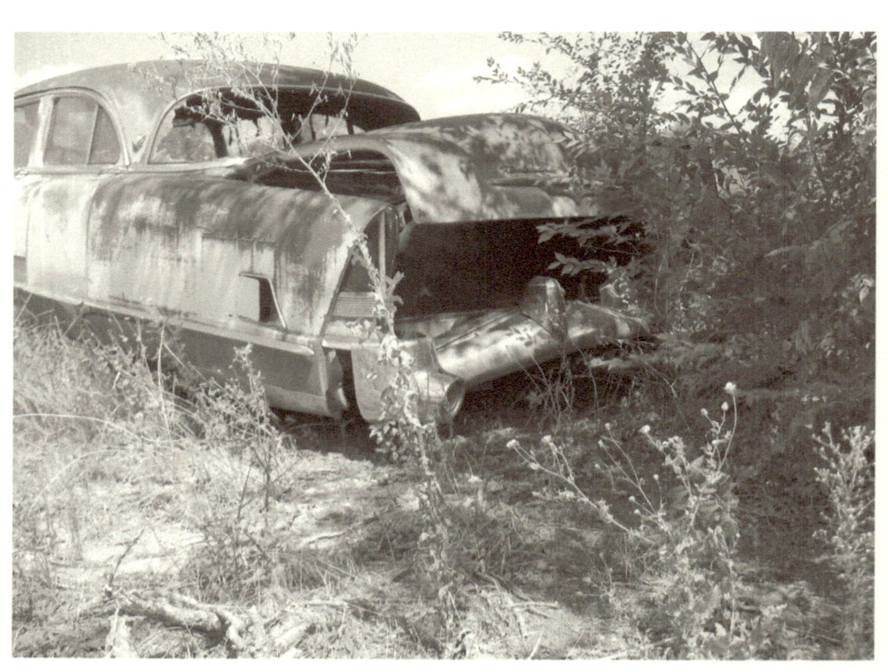

Relatives, Portraits, Then as Now

Charles, 1942

Uncle Mick,
gangly and young,
carried my four year old
father on his shoulders.
My grandmother led
the way across the field,
while she beat the
waist-high grasses
with a stick to
scare the snakes.

A storm is coming.
They hike west,
into blue and dust,
like pilgrims and pioneers.
Jess Ware has a dugout.
He does not bathe, and
mold grows in the
corners of his dirt floor.
They listen, wait. Wind
pushes down the earth,
lightning scars,
blackjacks alight with
dark smoke.

Caroline, Summer Night, 1947

I imagine she heard cicadas chattering
in prairie grasses uncut since they'd
drunk away the ancient salt sea. She sat
on the porch and listened. I imagine it
was thick night, prickled with drought
and dim stars, while she waited out the
vigilante family of a country man
to deliver on their intent as stated in the
street outside Hick's Department Store.
She suspected they might try fire this time,
a plan rich in its viciousness: to trap
her at the end of the neighborless
county road.

She didn't burn any lamps so that the pitch
was her advantage. She kept her ears attuned for
wheels slicing along the dirt road, the crunch of
cinder under a man's boot, coyotes barking
at fresh scents. There was nothing yet
but the skitter of grasshoppers skulking up
through the weeds. Her fate was public,
lived between suspicion and gratitude, a
symptom of marriage to the only lawman
of the Stephens County court. She received
as many curses on her name as she did
food tins left at her door.

Her son slipped like a breath onto the
porch and she put her finger to her lips.
She had readied them both, the chance to run
of too great a value compared to innocence.
At supper she'd told him to sleep in his
jeans and that she didn't want to hear how
hot. *If I holler for you to hie to the
creek*, she said, *you go*. A little boy but
too smart to think they anticipated storms

just because she'd put his shoes next to
the bed while he slept. She let him stand there
a long time while the .44 balanced on her lap,
drew bobby pins from her apron pocket,
and made curls. They listened
uncertain from which direction
their imaginings might come.

Rusty, 1981

We rode to the farm in the bed of the red Chevy.
Neither of us had the inclination for cattle or oil,
most especially the heat. But the drone of the highway
east of town romanced us. We picked stalks of oat
grass because we liked the green scent of it. We
leaned our backs against the cab and offered the stalks
out like Roman candles, grain heads scattering like
sparks on the wind. The farm lay in a wash a thousand
acres long. King snakes secreted their long bodies
into every precious crevice on that prairie. We
hunted up sticks to kill them but Daddy wouldn't
let us. Said they kept the rats out of the hay. We
were never as fascinated with the place as we were
with getting there. Cows called, calves counted, salt
licks chipped down, and we were done. Space got the
best of us. We dripped Strawberry Fanta (if we remembered
to save any from the ride out) on the backs of scorpions
(if we were lucky enough to find any). Then we sat under
the tailgate out of the sun. Horny toads spun around our
feet, impressing trails in the sand. It never occurred to us
he was working. Or that we would forget the way there.
But then we thought that was all there was to it.

My Mother's Lessons in Cooking Are About Her Mother

In one of the Dakotas, then near a vineyard in
California, she worked in the weary boarding
houses. Handwork and bleach, the best made
of shabby situations. It was want defined in a
language foreign in my generation.

Poverty is relative, then as now. The needfulness
of the life absorbed her, so that she never smiled
in photographs, though my other granny said she
was the lady and remarked her white gloves.

A handful of flour recounts much for my mother,
prompts her to tell me to go by when it looks right.
I stumble on approximation, no matter how simple
or stupid. Yet all that's asked of me is to live with
what's been done for me, worried out on my behalf.

Too many of my women before me went without
specifics for me to be complaining now. Work got
done at the cost of sleep and frayed skin, without the
mathematics of directions. What remains for me to
do is trust a dough mixed by my hand will rise the
way she said it would.

Travel to me is a trope, reinvention by words, an
empty means of play, while my grandmother never
went from the boarding house into the city. Tables
waited to be laid with plates, and the job stayed
the same, one day and again the next.

Contest

Two men stop my father as he wheels the baler in the pasture farthest from the barn. They lean on the bed of a new blue Ford, wear pearl snap shirts, and gesture with clean hands. It's evening. There's a lot of hay left to bale. My father doesn't like them already.

"They sure got you out late," one of the men says, and the other laughs like it's a joke. My father, however, keeps his thoughts out of the conversation. A kennel box in the bed of the truck holds three greyhound dogs, "purebloods," one of the men is fast to say. They slobber and whine while these men tell my father he's got it all wrong. What it's like when you own the land. My father doles them patience they fail to comprehend.

They are not the first to tell him what it's like to be a working man. He counts bales on the landscape, feels in his shirt pocket for his half-smoked cigar. He is the first to notice the coyote come out of the trees. "Well," one of the men drawls," look what we got here."

It's clear he feels this opportunity comes straight from God to prove all he means, that's how certain the look he gives my father. The coyote inventories the grouping of men and dogs, from the perspective of the outnumbered and overpowered. "You're about to see a good takedown, Charles. These here are good running dogs," they say and take the tailgate down.

My father leans back in the baler's chair and relights the cigar. He nods to show he's interested. The men and their dogs blow excited breath. It'd be enough to cause panic, if you didn't know what was coming, the way those dogs set on the coyote. He stays firm until a point in time of only his knowing, then he plows off through the Johnson grass, through the tallest thickest stalks, his race strong but clearly slower than the dogs'. "We got you now, you son of bitch." The two men laugh. "Yeah, we got you now."

The coyote's too maligned, been accused of too much, and these men and dogs have counted on this falsity. He knows the land they claim deeper than the curve of its surface. He's been run down too many times. Nature's bred out all the sick and the dumb. He lets the greyhounds gain then he sails up, a gray arc on the skyline, and folding his legs beneath him, dives headlong into the copse. There's a great thrashing of dogs in the tall grasses and a distant yelp.

The little cavalry reconstitutes and proceeds south with new fury. Another quarter-mile those dogs screech on. When it's quiet again, the coyote's head emerges from the grass. He watches the dogs over the horizon, till they're deep and gone, before casting his consideration back to the men.

The coyote shakes off the chaff and sets off at a trot, angling back down his original course. "Yeah," my father says, "them are some good running dogs," and plunges the baler back into action, all matters of certainty settled for the day.

Ass-Kickin' Red-Neck Bitch *

She comes banging into the parking lot of the Gas-N-Go, long straight hair flying while she saws on the wheel of her third-hand Silverado. Leaves it running, windows down, and when you see her blue-devil toenails in flip-flops you realize you were expecting boots. She's a tiny thing, soft belly under the hem of her tank top letting you know she's tan all over. Inside she buys a cherry drink and two packs of cigarettes with money from her back pocket. Your best guess is somewhere between sixteen and forty. Against the expanse of summer she reads like constant motion, in a town too small to hold her. But she's staying here for lack of a duplicate geography and all the world doesn't provide her. She's looking at you, or at least you see yourself reflected small and slanted in her sunglasses, and you needn't be bothered how hard she'll get bumped going into the corners. For a second there you thought you had something to say, but whatever you'd say would just trickle down the high ridge of her back. When she's ready she'll rip loose, whether you're looking or not.

**Stencil on back window of white 80s model truck; April 2009*

To the Boy at the Round-Up Club Dance

I didn't expect to
be asked by you,
by anyone

to shuffle, or waltz

Ropers scraped along the
plywood dancefloor
catfish grease on the breeze

shuffle, then waltz

my fingers found the
sharp-cut edge
of your hair
above your collar

shuffle, waltz

I was at the beginning
of coming undone, of
some day waking up
to what I want

to waltz

Watermelons

We stop at the green pick-up backed down to the road,
where a spindly-looking stick of an old man sits
in a lawn chair next to the truck. The chair rests cock-eyed
on the lip of the ditch, the webbing stripped and flittering with the wind,
and I start the whole thing off with a bad feeling.
Farm stands along U.S. 81 south of Rush Springs
brim with the fruit of the watermelon capital of the world.
All but the one where my father has stopped.

The old man does not rise when we pull in, does not wave,
just hollers *three apiece* before we're a step from our car.
The watermelons are piled in the truck bed and spilled onto the tailgate.
Some have been smashed on the dirt,
ants of every color swimming in the sticky juice.
My father nods, says *hot enough for you*, but the old man
acts like we're not there.

A salt ring darkens his straw cowboy hat,
and his squared-off sunglasses are so black I think
maybe he doesn't much see us. He keeps gnarled hands with yellow nails
clasped over the front of his overalls. His skin is translucent in the heat.
Off to my side I hear my father turning the melons over,
thumping them here and there while I stare at my blank face reflected in the
grimy black plastic.

With a hard jerk the old man hisses *watch out for my god damn dog*
and he points at me.
I look on the ground around me for the dog I had not noticed before.
It lies in the shade of the tailgate,
cockleburs matted in its filthy white coat. It does not flinch
at the stinging black horse flies lighting on its face.
I'm pretty sure the dog is dead.

My father hands me a watermelon, puts another under his arm,
says *I got six dollars for two.*
Three apiece, I told you, god damn it. The old man waves a hand at us
like he's shooing those nasty flies. And my father, who doesn't take shit
from anybody about anything just says *well, I believe you're right,*
and drops three one dollar bills then, after a pause,
three more onto the tailgate.

The old man stands up and spits.
Brown juice and shreds of half-chewed tobacco dribble down his chin,
his overalls, and onto his hand. His picks up the money and sits back down
without wiping any of it off.
I look at the dog again, unmoving,
its fur soaking up pink juice from busted melons.

As we close in on town the farm stands are more frequent and more abundant.
They have bins and shelters and parking lots,
and they give customers boxes to put the produce in.
We pass a wooden watermelon on a flatbed trailer
lettered tightly with the words
yellow diamond/orange meat/cantaloupes/squash/beans/we have everything
and once the trailer is out of sight I ask my father
what was wrong with that dog.
He rests his arm in the open window, his eyes looking up the highway,
tells me the devil is everywhere.

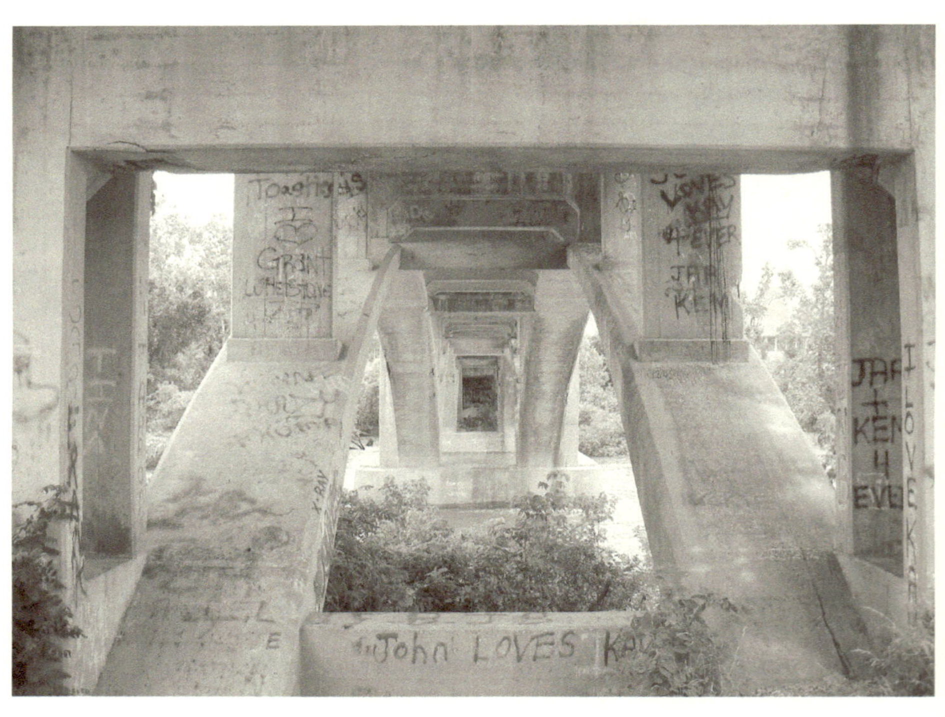
John LOVES

Highways Some Place Else

Maps to the Crash Sites

handwritten directions
on the margin
creases wearing
colored paper
an arrow pointing
to last coffee

a series of left
left again
then finally
right turns
black pick-up
guaranteed
to break down

nowhere
to buy food
on roads lined by
cement picnic tables
the world's largest
seismograph
on the world's
quietest fault
fewer riders
farther out

the legend is
one artist's
rendition so
one inch equals
one mile only
more-or-less

frequent need to
clean the windshield
dark by estimated
time of arrival
all borders porous
and negotiable

Maps, Pt. 2

I.

She begins building her system of signs when she
draws tiny hearts on her skin.

Before she knows it, she looks for a way of marking who she wants to be.

She owns something else, more complicated,
but tiny hearts are all she can draw with
clean edges.

Tattoos spell nothing natural.
She licks her thumb and wipes the hearts off.

II.

She draws lines on paper, jagged and long,
but where she meant to divide and separate she builds a border.

She is boxed in.

Lines put a shape to her that
make her recognizable,
a shape less fluid than she pretends.

III.

She hopes what she's left with means something.

She lays fingertips to her pulse,
traces veins from thumb to shoulder.

Her skin is a map. If she looks at the backs of her hands,
she sees where she has been.

She is a map of tricks and roads that go nowhere.

IV.

She gathers up pages covered in stains that cannot be erased.
She counts all she wishes
she did not know.

She is given a bone to scratch,
uses it to write in the dirt she brought with her.

Geography Lessons

Lesson 1
Find maps. They are everywhere. Signs with pictures. Arrows on boxes. Recipes. Dash lights. Pictographs on bathroom doors. Lines on the grocery store floor. Be amazed by all words can't say.

Lesson 2
Look at the kiosk telling you YOU ARE HERE. But when you look around your surroundings know they will resemble nothing from the map. A space opens between expectation and resolution. It is more often true that you just are where you are, rather than where you meant to be. Look forward to lost.

Lesson 3

Follow the flow to the front of the store where the old woman sits smack on one of those arrows on the floor that shows how traffic should flow through the automatic doors. Groceries spill from a white plastic bag. One orange bearing a Texas Citrus sticker rolls away from the lady and under a cluster of carts. The woman is surrounded. Gary-The-Checker holds her hand, pats her, says "Oh, honey. You know where you are, honey?" Look from the woman's face to the floor again. The path of the orange has cut a gleam into the dust. "I'm sitting right here, stupid," the old woman says, and you think you know what she means.

Lesson 4

Lying in bed at night maps will get the best of you. Feel the path your blood follows as it crosses over your heart. Patterns are everywhere. Hard not to be afraid of all the places your life doesn't go.

Things to Know Before You Leave on This Trip

The first aid kit is insufficient,
has never been opened,
is likely dead of old age.
West of here you get the
farm report on the radio;
south west of here, nothing.
Girl Scouts carry lighters
and pen knives and more
evidence you are unprepared.

You are guaranteed to take
a wrong turn, to be short toll money,
to have packed the wrong clothes.
Nowhere isn't on the page,
you won't know it when you get there,
but you will after you leave.
Crave meaningful directions,
just don't expect them when you ask.
Spend your map money on tacos
and those chips that come in a can,
clean ice for the cooler every day.
You'll see lawn ornaments, dozens
if not hundreds, and God help you
if you ever figure out that why.
Wave at everyone you pass
on a two-lane road because that's
what we do out here. Say something
to everyone who speaks to you.
Look them in the eye like you're
asking them for money. Register
that everybody's got some place
they need to go.

Everyone Left Texas

There's nobody on watch in the hill country.

They're all out on those roads that run straight
and flat except for when they ride you up over
a plain.

I met up with them at that café you like
because the waitresses are all old and fat and
everything smells like cherry and Tabasco.

We all got to talking, it was the funniest thing,
as if borders can dematerialize, like place is
just a state of being.

Louisiana

On the way out we stayed
in a house by the river.
Walls wept through pink paper
and the windows all held box fans
that whined night and day.
The boy down the hall
could not keep from stirring.
Mertie called to him,
put your head down, now,
but the beds were too hot
for any of us to sleep.
And so we inclined
ears toward the door
when Mertie finally said
he should at least
sing softer.
Next morning we left,
no one said goodbyes,
and drove north on a road
lined with guineas.
They tumbled and roiled,
like leaves in strong wind,
more casualties
in the wake.
I wanted to say how funny
but couldn't,
and so said nothing
about guineas or the speed of life.
It all got left in a Motel 6
with the questions of when
and the decision just to go.
Up the high tide line we skimmed
over all that lay
between us and the water.

Carl Junction, Missouri, Two Nights After 4th of July

The ache resides here always and as sweet as it is,
as much like home as it feels, it isn't what you were
hoping for. Because you make a u-turn on Hillcrest,
you are the curiosity of the policeman waiting in the
dark parking lot of what was until a month ago the
skating rink. You are an easy, quiet, momentary
scandal in a simple, sleeping town on the last cool
night expected for months.

The red star above the fire station, remnant of Christmas,
is alight amid holiday residue. The other side of town
isn't town so much as it is rows of vinyl-sided houses,
identical and square in a way that makes you feel dry.
The plains intersect the hills, officially and in some
rare definition, a geological truth you're considerably
certain no one in those houses knows. The only reason
they made this home is because once the trains stopped here,
a depot for putting cattle on and off, but nonetheless a
purpose ambitious beyond a golf course.

When you reach downtown, all block and half of it, the
policeman gives you up for a few too-young-to-drive
teenagers on the bench in front of the drugstore. Or maybe
it's the two on bikes popping wheelies against the curb at
the convenience store. You are the only one out driving
just to be driving, because there was a song on the radio and
used to be that when your song came on the radio you had to
keep driving because God only knew when they'd play it again.
God only knew what any of us was bound to do.

Breakdown

What we wanted, we said, was to drink
and dance on tables. Girls turned loose in
the summer time. Told everyone we saw
we were leaving, then went out and made
bad time on roads we knew. We wanted
the freedom that comes with driving, but
our lives were absent the longing. Little
surprise we went lost so early on.

In a Motel 6 in North Little Rock we
listened as a man beat a woman on the
sidewalk by the pool. She screamed hit
me again, her hair like glowing snakes.
We left when the police came. Windows
opened up to the blue night, smelling
honeysuckle the whole way. Gone, like
we were the ones running.

We plum lost eighty dollars, traded a
watch for beer. Found only one clean
McDonald's bathroom. Two weeks of
bitching and baloney on white bread,
Linney put her head down on a cement
picnic table and bawled. She was the
only rich girl any of us knew.

You can't say where on the map we
drowned. Crossing a border somewhere.
We got sopped up by the humidity and
stagnant air. We all felt it but didn't say
it, the way lost people never do. We kept
stopping at state lines, sleepy and faded
in every picture, none of us friends by the
time we hit Kansas.

Displacement

I idled at an intersection in Nevada,
or New Mexico, watched some guy
pushing WALK and thought:
everywhere is somewhere, right?

I drove eighty miles to look at a wheat field.
I missed them and knew where one was.
Trespassed in Kansas. Cut under a canopy of trees
I couldn't name. If that had been back home I
would have said "blackjack."

Sidetracked into Missouri, the border deceptively
porous, and once there I had to do the job. I laid
breadcrumbs down the interstate. Eaten up by birds,
wind, storms.

If You Go at All (Directions to Comanche)

Scenic route, in the morning,
best way to go. Takes longer
but at speed you can handle.
Star-shaped motel signs, busted,
almost all. Slip over the edge
of town, into the edge of
the next. Borders not so fine as
you might think. In 300 miles
the storm will start, and nothing
else will name where you been.
It's WPA highway,
concrete slab on slab.
Listen and you'll drown:
run–cut & run–cut & run.

Locating Her

she fell into the space
between true and north

sought balms and salves
and things that heal
felt it all, so literal
she wrote it on her skin
made it of mud

put the soil in her mouth
so that it said
what she always meant to say

she's there,
on the plains,
her bones laid out under
the surface of iron sand
grains lifting

leaving
on constant winds
scattering to those
who know what it is
to live on this place

Space Makes Itself Known

You remember the day you first noticed.
The door to Clear Creek Diner opened,
and it blew on in. It pushed against your back
where you sat at one of the tables in the center aisle,
pushed just hard enough that you lurched forward
a little. Your hand dropped, spilling scrambled egg
from your fork. You turned to catch its eye before
the door closed again, but you could not see it. No
one could. That was a Tuesday in June, 8:47 in the
morning, Central Standard Time.

You felt it lurking for a while after that. Things
rustled in the periphery. You heard creaks.
Occasionally there were hiccups in the spinning
of the earth. You were suspicious. You never
turned a corner if curious shadows slipped around it,
were never the first to enter through a strange door
if you could help it. Once, sitting in your living room
at night, you saw a red face cast against your window.
You stared until you were assured there had
never really been a face.

Then came the first time gravity failed you.
You were getting out of bed, swung your legs
over the mattress, but your feet did not touch
the floor. So you tumbled out, leaden and dazed,
feeling the fool for missing the floor. But then you knew:
the floating had started, the next signal of the expansion.
You hunted up a brick–compact but heavy–to help
weigh yourself down, but it was just a matter of time.
You were a sheaf of loose pages in need of a
cosmic paperweight.

Reading a book of poems you come across the line
"The apple draws the earth as well as the earth
draws the apple–Newton." The fingers of expansion
nag you daily, peel at your edges, pry you off your place
of scraggly trees and desperate wind. No architecture can
keep you in, and physics is too tenuous to explain.
You feel it waiting for you to confess, to swallow you whole.

Stasis

Crows scatter down
chants and caws,
remind me where I
diverged from the map.

One rides down
to consider me
at close range.

He wallows in the rocks,
kicks loose the renegades
hidden in my garden.

Out spin three
in succession,
each stone just
bigger than the last.

He tucks at wilding feathers
in need of rearranging,
sidesteps within inches of me,
all the while staring west-southwest.

We consider the solidity,
the wear, the rub
of each rock.
We are both thinking
of taking flight.

Prairie Sickness

She feels it at night, mostly,
and sometimes in her car
crossing empty railroad tracks,
the rush made by rocks
falling into ravines and
granite whittling buried
mountains.

While she works she awaits a
feast of wild plums made from
trees in her yard, descendants of
those eaten by salt and erosion.

She feels the constant, faulting
geology disturbing the surface
of the cut-off sea sunken
through the shale below her.
With her eyes closed she feels a
motion, a sickness, like floating.

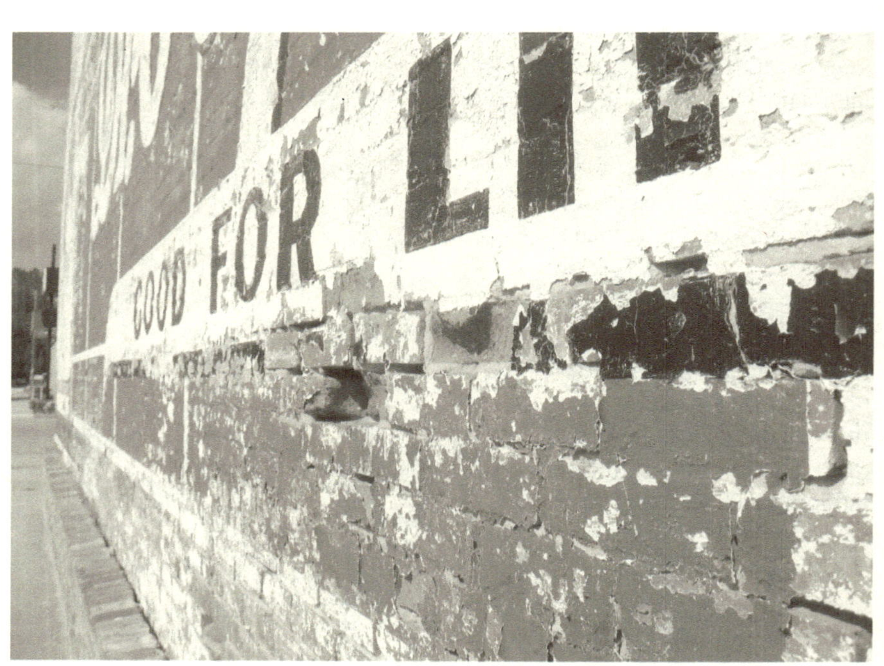
GOOD FOR

July

July

I.

They're talking about dancing, seems like,
nearly everybody in town. But this time
of year, when the heat withers you through,
dancing is just a dream. We're settled in that
space between independence and the end of
time, where all anybody can think is
how quiet it is these days. Feet are slick
on the floorboards. Old metal doorknobs
try catching at their latches. You're lingering,
but you don't remember what for.

Later today it will rain, but so thin and
pitiful boys working on their cars won't even
come inside. It'll shine up the asphalt for a
while. Blink and you just might cry. Wait for
it to be evening, and for the radio to
play something good.

2.

Heck's stepmother used to take Polaroids of him
whenever he left the house. This was when he was
little. She placed him in front of the white wall of
the entry way so his clothes and hair stood out. Some
times her hands shook when she held the camera up,
Heck fidgeting so his elbows knocked against the wall.
That summer he was old enough to ride his bike to the
creek alone, and Heck's father yelled at his wife to let
the boy go on. So she stopped, and for a while after
Heck lingered by the front door a little while extra
every time he went out. His stepmother sat near a
window all day, the light coming in enough to bake
her. Smoked whole cartons of cigarettes, the house
weighted down by the haze. When she hadn't changed
her housecoat for three days and no one could recall
when last she spoke, Heck's dad put her in the car.
From there she smiled at Heck, her head lolling on the
headrest, pressed her fingertips to the window glass
like a sleepy kid. They drove away, but she
never came back. Heck sees himself in her shoe
box of Polaroids still hidden in the dresser, her thousands
of fingerprints touching his face.

3.

Mary's skin is always damp and salty, her
fingers always sticky with dirt. She never
feels clean enough wearing her church dresses.
Often when she stands with other women she
hears herself emitting compliments and sweetness
she doesn't feel. But she's the worker. She's
meant to sound grateful.

4.

Gracie tastes beer and salt. She's always got that
sloe-eyed look about her, the one that keeps people
from noticing her eyes are burned-out and blue.
She can't conceive of herself in any kind of detail
except when she's alone. Then she thinks of lists
of things she'd like to say, but that she doesn't. She's
pretty sure no one would believe it's her.

5.

Girls are laying out on the slant of the
roof next door. They've got a bedroom
window open, music too old for them to know
playing. Can't hold still, not a-one of
them, on a day so hot birds won't fly. They're
living in slow motion, waiting for the song
to change, thinking maybe it's
true no one ever leaves.

6.

Heck's best friend Donny Jr. says "where'd
your mamma go?" They're at the fort: a bank of
thick, flat rocks that slope into the creek. Heck
likes that the rocks are as big as rooms and the way
the hackberries shade them like a roof. He's looking
at a crevice in the rock he claims as his, and
at the hundreds of pebbles residing in it. "She's
in heaven, I guess." He pinches some pebbles
out and arranges them on the rock by size.
He waits while Donny Jr. takes in his lie like
a fact or any other rule, waits for a kind and
quiet "yeah." Heck's not sure anymore when
he's supposed to go home, so he keeps on with
the sorting. Donny Jr. uses a stick to manage the
order of the pebbles. It keeps thundering and
not raining.

7.

Nobody's going in at the skating rink, so the girl
who runs it sits on the parking lot railing. She's
looked at the magazine in her hands so many
times there's nothing left to do but rip the pages
out one at a time. She's had all of the Eagles-on-a-loop
and no air conditioning she can stand. If a car will just
slow up some she'll hitch into town. When the clouds
begin to stir she prays it'll come a tornado or
some other thrill, some kind of cleaver to
gut open the day. The scattered magazine pages
catch on a rough wind, but she doesn't see them
leave for the white sun blinding the world. Someone
coming down the highway honks, but it's not enough
to fill the space.

8.

Mary's washing dishes, thinking what her sister
might be doing. She's scraping burnt potatoes out
of a pan, poking at them, useless, with a fork.
There's Gracie, who's plucked her eyebrows bald
and paints her face brighter than natural. Mary's
kitchen window frames the neighbor's house and
a yard needing mowing. Mary's washing dishes,
waiting for dusk to fall so all the flies
will light somewhere else for the night. She's
thinking about her sister, and about driving to Tulsa
that time, her flying hair, wearing her favorite shirt
and how that El Camino driver didn't even look over.
About Gracie and lipstick and gravity and how it was
hard to say just how, but all those things went together.

9.

Gracie points clients to the casino's change machines,
but she daydreams about places a way on down the road.
She worries about the distance between here
and what would be better. And it's a waste of time
to say how filthy gas station bathrooms are,
how the lights click and buzz and cast yellow
sickness on her skin. "Mary, Mary, Mary,"
she says out loud. "How far is far from home?
How long till I get gone?" Never been a girl
more miserable in her own skin. Gracie wants
to sigh, but none of what's eating her will leave her.

10.

They're just boys practicing all the ways they're
going to be. Smiles to look like they know things
that are only ideas to them. The way they hold cigarettes,
pinched between their fingertips so as not to hold their
smokes like some girls. You'd miss them, these boys,
if they left out of town, in their t-shirts with the sleeves
cut out, red tans, sitting in their pickups with the
windows always down. Smelling like musk and hay,
throwing loops at sawhorses, thinking they'll do more
than their daddies can. They stretch out the size of
their strides. Got all the ingredients to be who you
want them to be. You're broken in your heart,
so pretty are these boys.

II.

Heck's father is building a cabinet in the
garage. A ring of sawdust sticks to the skin
around his shirt collar. When Heck asks him how
it can thunder so long before a rain, Heck's dad only
says "if it wants to rain, let it." Down at the fort
the wind is finally picking up and has washed all the
pebbles to the ground. A granddaddy long-legs
comes up through the crevice, and Heck takes
him in his hand. He twists his arm, and the spider
stretches gray legs from one of Heck's fingers
to another. When the wind of the new storm
threatens to catch him, he flexes and
rides the weather.

12.

Sulphur from the oil leases coats every breath.
Between that and the heat a person could choke.
But it's Friday, so Ila Lee goes to get her hair
done at the beauty shop next to the phone office.
Dogs push at every door that opens, and you
sympathize at how bad they want in. Nobody's
outside to help Ila Lee up the curb. They're in the
diner watching condensation on the glasses sweat
the flavor out of whatever they're drinking.

Riding out on the edge of town you hear
the chain link fence at the baseball field clanking
with the wind. When the road ends at the highway
there's not even a stop sign, but you wait. You
had a notion to go somewhere, but there's no telling
how long that's been.

Wind

It’s a state line thing
a plains thing.

The way I breathe there,
the way I’m prompted to lay my fingertips
to the curves of my ribcage.

Smell of iron,
grit sifted into my clothes,
stains in every water-colored layer of red.

How it catches the thistle in its attitude,
rides tin roofs into metal fatigue.

It’s home on my skin,
a day not washed off with soap and water.

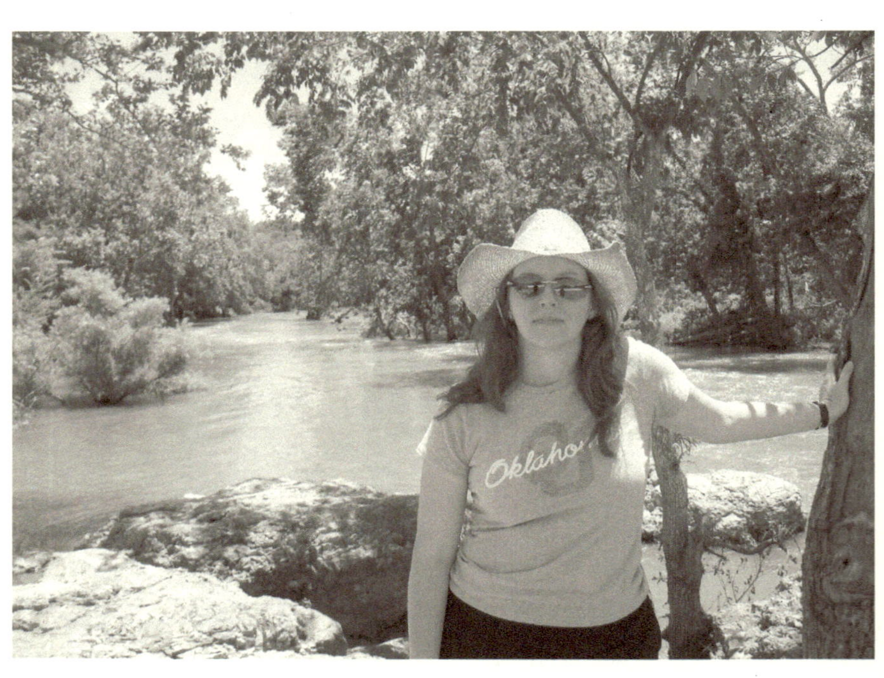
Oklaho

Joey Brown has spent much of her life so far in a car traveling the spaces between the towns of Oklahoma. She's put much of what she's seen and heard along the way in these poems. She's written other poems and short stories that have appeared in literary journals across the country including *Rhino*, *Quiddity*, *Westview*, *The Mid-America Poetry Review*, *storySouth*, and *The Florida Review*. Her poetry has been nominated for the Pushcart Prize. Brown is a writing professor and holds an MA in Creative Writing and a Ph.D. in Interdisciplinary Studies from the University of Oklahoma. She is currently living in southwest Missouri.

www.ingramcontent.com/pod-product-compliance
Lightning Source LLC
LaVergne TN
LVHW051019080826
845145LV00009B/2694

* 9 7 8 0 9 8 0 1 6 8 4 6 4 *